This coloring book belongs to:

_____

_____

Live Laugh FUCK OFF

ADULT SWEAR WORDS COLORING BOOK

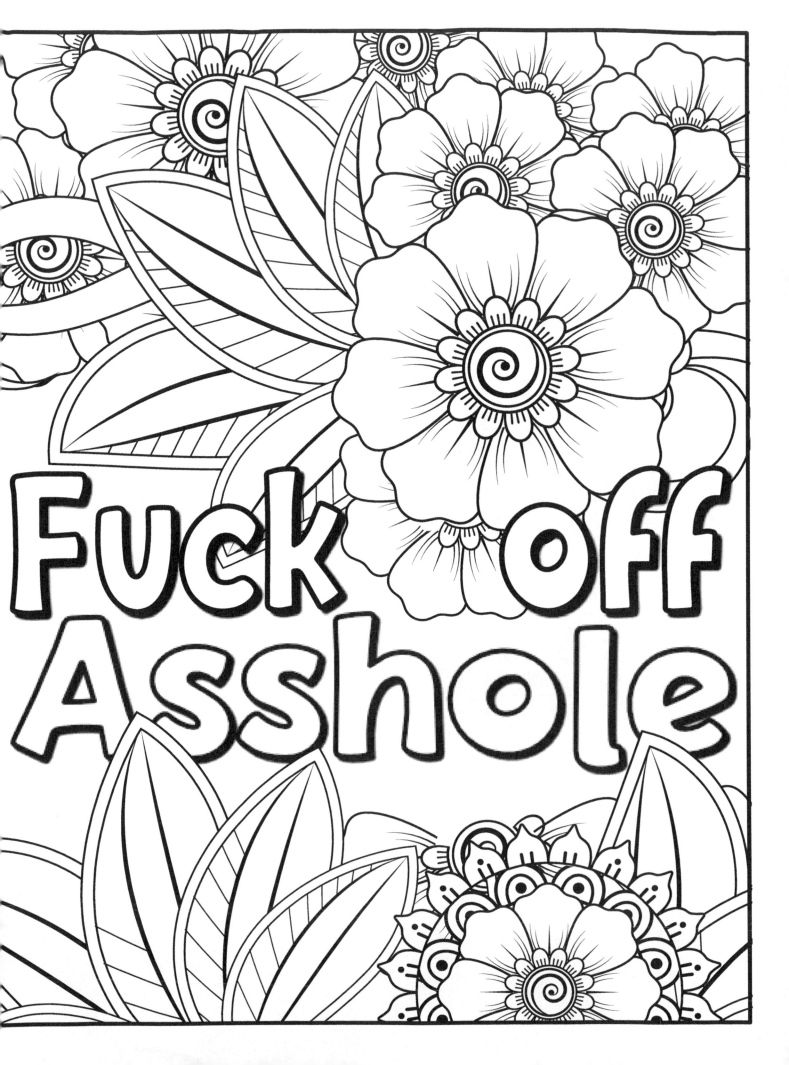

Roses are red
Violets are
...
nvm
Fuck you!

There's so much *Fuckery* to spread

BE FUCKING HAPPY

Color testing page

Color testing page

Printed in Great Britain
by Amazon

28733349R00051